W9-CDL-301

Basic Skills

Guided Writing

Encourages Writing Skills and Creative Thinking

Grade 3

By
Patricia Howard

Cover Artist
Matthew Van Zomeren

Inside Illustrations by
Marty Bucella

Published by Instructional Fair • TS Denison
an imprint of

 **McGraw-Hill**
Children's Publishing

About the Author

Patricia Howard has a degree in Primary Education with a focus on teaching children with special needs. She has taught for more than thirty years at all levels of education, from kindergarten through twelfth grade. She has a wide range of experience, from teaching in a classroom setting to being a tutor for homebound children. Pat believes in a holistic approach to education and individualized instruction to accommodate students' needs. Pat is the author of *Word Problems Grades 2–3*. She currently lives in British Columbia, Canada.

Credits

Author: Patricia Howard
Inside Illustrator: Marty Bucella
Cover Design: Matthew Van Zomeren
Project Director/Editor: Mary Rose Hassinger
Editors: Alyson Kieda, Kathryn Wheeler
Graphic Layout: Tracy L. Wesorick

In loving memory
of my big brother, friend, and soul mate,
Keith Howard.
1945–1997

McGraw-Hill
Children's Publishing

A Division of The McGraw·Hill Companies

Published by Instructional Fair • TS Denison
An imprint of McGraw-Hill Children's Publishing
Copyright © 2002 McGraw-Hill Children's Publishing

Limited Reproduction Permission: Permission to duplicate these materials is limited to the person for whom they are purchased. Reproduction for an entire school or school district is unlawful and strictly prohibited.

Send all inquiries to:
McGraw-Hill Children's Publishing
3195 Wilson Drive NW
Grand Rapids, Michigan 49544

All Rights Reserved • Printed in the United States of America

Guided Writing—grade 3
ISBN: 0-7424-0229-0

3 4 5 6 7 8 9 PHXBK 07 06 05 04 03

Table of Contents

Note to the Teacher

Guided Writing provides creative springboards for writing instruction which may otherwise have had the class staring at blank sheets of writing paper, searching for ideas to impress the reader and/or the teacher. This is a book with a dual purpose: to stimulate and motivate creative thinking and to guide students toward confident written expression of those thoughts.

Students can often be daunted by the writing process with all its various requirements—proper punctuation, complete sentences, topic statements, and detail statements. Sometimes these considerations stifle original thoughts and even enthusiasm for the writing process itself. The creative thinking exercises provided in *Guided Writing* give opportunities for young writers to generate their own ideas rather than to retrieve information from carefully chosen resources. Students are not required to come up with predetermined answers—in fact, different responses to the same question are encouraged and expected.

There are four statements or questions on each page. The first three guide the student toward a particular theme, providing thought-provoking ideas that will stimulate the imagination. Each of the statements, while related in some way, will take the student beyond the actual theme, challenging flexibility in thinking. The student can then use these original ideas to form solidly written paragraphs, following your curriculum's writing process.

This concept of developing independent creative thinkers and writers will take time and patience. Students need to build confidence in themselves and their ideas, and they need to strengthen their ability to take risks and do their own thinking. Some of your writers may even have difficulty letting go of their need for always having the "right" answer. However, with the activities in this book, students will find a creative vehicle for practicing and strengthening these essential thinking and writing skills. The process will help them to become the fluent and creative writers and thinkers that we hope all of our students grow to be.

Name_____

The Dragon Next Door

How might your neighborhood be different if there were a dragon living next door?

_____

_____

_____

List three good things and three bad things about having a dragon for a pet.

_____

_____

_____

_____

Why do you think dragons have fiery breath? _____

_____

_____

Describe a dragon.

_____

_____

_____

_____

_____

Name_____

If Feet Were Round

Why are feet rectangular and not round or square? _____

_____

_____

Why do you think we have toes? How are they useful? _____

_____

_____

How might your life be different if you had three feet? _____

_____

_____

_____

_____

Describe feet.

_____

_____

_____

_____

_____

_____

_____

Rainbow

How do you think rainbows feel, smell, and sound? _____

_____

_____

Where do you think rainbows end? _____

_____

_____

Give some examples of what you might do with a rainbow if you could catch one.

_____

_____

_____

Describe a rainbow.

_____

_____

_____

_____

_____

_____

Name_____

Why Exercise?

How do you feel after running for ten minutes?_____

_____

Name some of the exercises you have done. _____

_____

_____

If you never exercised, what might happen to you? _____

_____

_____

_____

Why do people exercise?

_____

_____

_____

_____

_____

_____

_____

_____

Name_____

The Apple of My Eye

Who are the people you like the most? Why? _____

_____

_____

What are five things you like about one of your classmates or close friends?

_____

_____

_____

Parents often call their children names like "sweetie pie." What are some other nice names you have heard?

_____

_____

_____

Explain the meaning of the phrase "You're the apple of my eye."

_____

_____

_____

_____

_____

_____

Name_____

Word Wonder

List six words you think are more fun pronounced backwards.

_____

_____

List five words you think could be spelled an easier way. Spell them both ways in your list.

_____

_____

_____

List all the meanings that you know for the word **run**.

_____

_____

_____

ZONG TWINGLE TS PO ARB BLIRP YUZ NG

If you could speak only fifteen words, what words would you choose?

_____

_____

_____

_____

_____

_____

Name_____

Goose Bumps

Why do you think we don't get goose bumps on our faces?

_____

_____

Tell about the last time you had goose bumps. _____

_____

_____

Do geese and other animals get goose bumps? Why or why not?

_____

_____

_____

What are goose bumps?

_____

_____

_____

_____

_____

_____

_____

Name_____

Antsy Ants

Why are there so many ants on sidewalks? _____

_____

_____

Why do people say that there are always ants at picnics? _____

_____

_____

_____

Describe what your day might be like if you were an ant. _____

_____

_____

_____

_____

Why do you think ants are so strong?

_____

_____

_____

_____

_____

_____

_____

_____

Name_____

Seeing Things

What are four things you can see with your eyes? _____

_____

What would it be like to have x-ray vision? _____

_____

_____

_____

What are five things you can see in the dark? _____

_____

_____

_____

How might your life be different without the use of your eyes?

_____

_____

_____

_____

_____

_____

_____

_____

Houses and Homes

Why doesn't everyone and everything live in the same type of home?

_____

_____

_____

What are five places that animals or people call home?

_____

_____

Describe what life would be like if you carried your home on your back like a turtle.

_____

_____

_____

What is a habitat? Describe some habitats.

_____

_____

_____

_____

_____

_____

_____

Name_____

Why Do We Read?

How would you explain reading to an alien? _____

_____

What is the best or most interesting thing you have ever read? Why?

_____

_____

How do you think the first person who could read learned to do so?

_____

_____

_____

_____

Why is being able to read so important?

_____

_____

_____

_____

_____

_____

_____

Name_____

Inventive Inventions

How do you think people come up with new ideas? _____

_____

_____

Describe the kind of person who invents things. _____

_____

_____

Give three examples of new inventions that would be useful today.

_____

_____

_____

_____

_____

What is an invention?

_____

_____

_____

_____

_____

_____

The Longest Hour

If you could add an extra hour to your day, how would you use it and why?

_____

_____

_____

Why do you think the hour hand on a clock is shorter than the minute hand?

_____

_____

Describe four of the most favorite times in your life. _____

_____

_____

_____

What seems like the longest hour of your day? Why?

_____

_____

_____

_____

_____

_____

Name_____

Starstruck

Explain what you think stardust is. _____

_____

_____

If wishing on a star worked, what would you wish for? Why? _____

_____

What do you suppose keeps stars from falling out of the sky? _____

_____

_____

Describe a star.

_____

_____

_____

_____

_____

_____

_____

Name_____

High in the Sky

What do you think a cloud is made of? _____

_____

_____

Why do you think clouds often form interesting shapes?

_____

_____

_____

Why do some clouds become storm clouds and others not?

_____

_____

_____

Describe the kind of home you would have to build if you lived on a cloud.

_____

_____

_____

_____

_____

_____

Name_____

Handy-Dandy

How does someone become right- or left-handed? _____

_____

_____

Do you think animals are right- or left-handed? _____

_____

_____

Describe what it might be like if you decided to use the hand opposite the one you usually use.

_____

_____

_____

_____

Why are some people left-handed and others right-handed?

_____

_____

_____

_____

_____

_____

Name_____

Games Galore

List five games that more than one person must play.

_____

_____

Name the game and then describe how you might change the rules of the last game you played with a friend.

_____

_____

_____

What makes one game exciting to play and another boring?_____

_____

_____

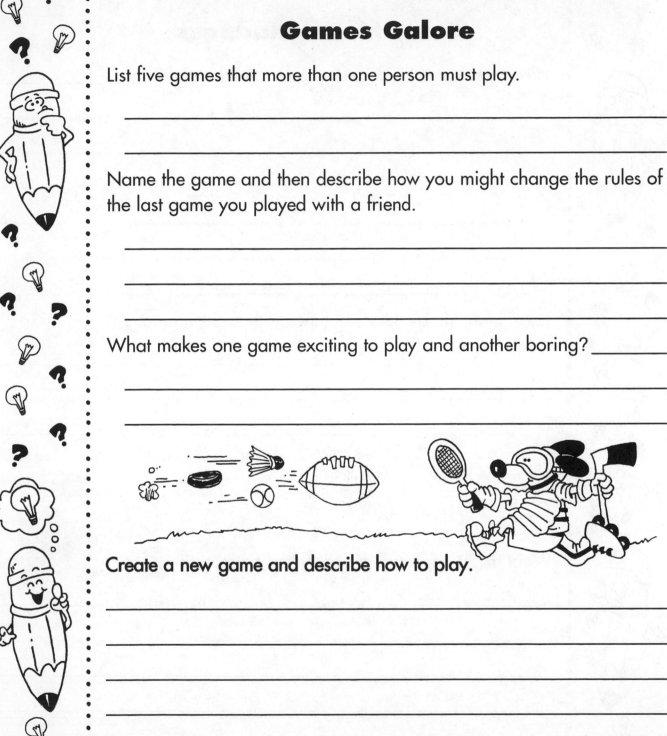

Create a new game and describe how to play.

_____

_____

_____

_____

_____

_____

_____

Moon Madness

Where do you think the moon goes during the day?

_____

_____

Who is the "man in the moon?"

_____

_____

_____

How might life be different if the earth had ten moons?

_____

_____

_____

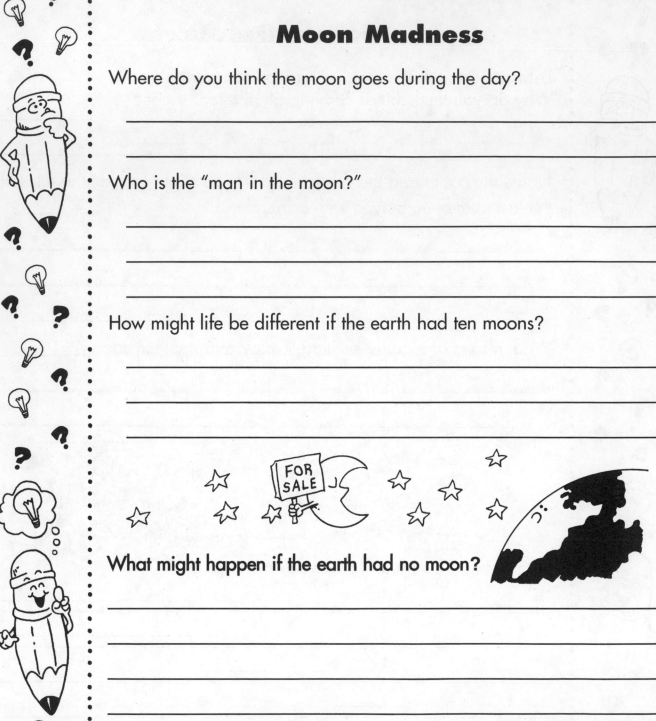

What might happen if the earth had no moon?

_____

_____

_____

_____

_____

_____

_____

Name_____

A Four-Corner World

Why do you think things come in all different shapes?

_____

_____

What is the best shape? Why? _____

_____

_____

Name all the things you can think of that are round.

_____

_____

_____

What would it be like if everything was square?

_____

_____

_____

_____

_____

_____

_____

© McGraw-Hill Children's Publishing IF5027 *Guided Writing*

Black and White

List as many objects as you can that are black and white. _____

_____

_____

Select three objects from your list and describe them, including what you do with them.

_____

_____

_____

What is your favorite black and white thing? Why?

_____

_____

Why are most soccer balls black and white?

_____

_____

_____

_____

_____

_____

_____

_____

Spider Fright

How might you help yourself get over a fear of spiders? _____

_____

_____

What effect do ladybugs and butterflies have on you? Why?

_____

_____

How would life be different if you had no fears? _____

_____

_____

_____

_____

EEK!

Why are some people afraid of spiders?

_____

_____

_____

_____

_____

_____

_____

Hard-to-Spell Words

List six words you think are hard to spell, and show how you would change them.

_____

_____

_____

_____

Why are some people good spellers and others not?

_____

_____

_____

Suggest two new spelling rules. _____

_____

_____

Why are some words so hard to spell?

Dixsionairy
Dikshuneri
Dicshinary
Di

_____

_____

_____

_____

_____

Hair Care

Why do you think the hair on your head grows longer than the hair in your eyebrows?

_____

_____

_____

Why doesn't it usually hurt to cut your hair? _____

_____

_____

Why do you think most people have hair on their heads?

_____

_____

_____

Why do many boys have their hair cut short?

_____

_____

_____

_____

_____

_____

_____

Neckties

Describe an outfit you like to wear.

_____

_____

_____

How might men's lives be different if neckties had not been invented?

_____

_____

Why do you think women often wear dresses and men most often wear pants?

_____

_____

_____

Why do many men wear neckties?

_____

_____

_____

_____

_____

_____

_____

Buttons, Clips, and Zips

Make two lists, one with things that have buttons and one with things that have zippers.

_____   _____

_____   _____

_____   _____

_____   _____

Describe how clothes might be fastened if buttons and zippers did not exist.

_____

_____

List four things used to fasten nonclothing items.

_____

_____

What is the easiest way to fasten clothing? Why?

_____

_____

_____

_____

_____

Wishful Thinking

If you had three wishes, what would they be?

_____

_____

_____

What might you do with a million dollars? _____

_____

_____

What might you do with your time if you didn't have to have a job?

_____

_____

_____

When making wishes, why do so many people hope for money?

_____

_____

_____

_____

_____

_____

Why Do We Have Vacations?

Describe an ideal vacation. _____

_____

_____

_____

Describe your best vacation and explain why it was the best.

_____

_____

_____

What are two advantages and two disadvantages to having school all year long?

_____

_____

_____

Why do most people go on vacations?

_____

_____

_____

_____

_____

New Year's Resolutions

How do you feel when a new year begins? _____

_____

_____

What is a resolution? What are three good things about making them?

_____

_____

_____

What changes might you make if you made and kept a New Year's resolution?

_____

_____

_____

Why do many people make New Year's resolutions?

_____

_____

_____

_____

_____

Why Do We Laugh?

Why does laughing make us feel good? _____

_____

_____

Describe a situation that would make you laugh. _____

_____

_____

What makes us want to be around funny people? _____

_____

_____

_____

HA HA HA HA HA HA

JOKES

Why do we laugh?

_____

_____

_____

_____

_____

_____

_____

Name_____

Do We Need Toes?

What might explain why one foot is often bigger than the other?

_____

_____

_____

What are two possible reasons for why toes are different lengths?

_____

_____

_____

What do you think might happen if we had square feet? _____

_____

_____

Why do people need toes?

_____

_____

_____

_____

_____

_____

Picture Perfect

How do you feel when you see a picture that you really like?

_____

_____

_____

Why do you think some paintings become very valuable?

_____

_____

How would you decorate your own house or apartment? Give three details.

_____

_____

_____

Why do we hang pictures in our homes and schools?

_____

_____

_____

_____

_____

_____

_____

Name_____

Why Do We Sleep?

What does it mean to dream? _____

_____

_____

Why do you suppose babies need more sleep than grownups?

_____

_____

Why causes us to wake up? Describe as many things as you can.

_____

_____

_____

Why do we sleep?

_____

_____

_____

_____

_____

Name_____

Birds of a Feather

What is the best thing about birds? _____

_____

_____

Why do you think some birds can talk and others cannot?

_____

_____

If you could be a bird, what kind would you be and why?

_____

_____

_____

Use your imagination to create a new kind of bird. Describe the bird in detail.

_____

_____

_____

_____

_____

_____

_____

Name_____

So Many Differences

Why do you think some people have great musical talent and others do not?

_____

_____

_____

Why do you think some children are short and others tall?

_____

_____

What would it be like if everyone had brown hair and freckles?

_____

_____

_____

Why do you think people are so different from each other?

_____

_____

_____

_____

_____

Name_____

Wink and Blink

What are four things that make you blink your eyes? _____

_____

_____

Why do you think we have tears when we cry? _____

_____

_____

Do you think feathers would work as well as eyelashes? Why?

_____

_____

_____

Why do some people wink?

_____

_____

_____

_____

_____

Name_____

Be a Bookworm

Why do you think some gardeners are said to have a "green thumb"?

_____

_____

_____

Have you ever had a nickname? What and why? _____

_____

_____

What nicknames might you give someone that was very creative?

_____

_____

_____

Why do we call people who love to read "bookworms"?

_____

_____

_____

_____

_____

_____

© McGraw-Hill Children's Publishing
IF5027 Guided Writing

Name_____

Favorite Foods

Why do you think hot dogs are a popular food? _____

_____

_____

Which tastes better, brussels sprouts or pizza? Why? _____

_____

_____

Explain how to prepare your favorite food. _____

_____

_____

_____

_____

If you could create your own recipe for a food, what would it be?

_____

_____

_____

_____

_____

_____

Name_____

Only Four Fingers

What might explain why horses have hooves? _____

_____

_____

Why do you think people have feet and not claws or paws?

_____

_____

Why do we have a baby toe even after we are grown up?

_____

_____

_____

Why do you think some cartoon characters have four fingers?

_____

_____

_____

_____

_____

Why Does an Octopus Have Eight Legs?

Why does a centipede need so many legs? _____

_____

_____

Why are kangaroos so good at hopping? _____

_____

_____

_____

What are four uses for legs, besides walking and running?

_____

_____

_____

Why does an octopus have eight legs?

_____

_____

_____

_____

_____

Rain, Rain, Go Away

Where do puddles go after the rain? _____

_____

Why do you think it rains more in some places than in others?

_____

_____

Describe what a flood must be like. _____

_____

_____

_____

_____

Why does it rain?

_____

_____

_____

_____

_____

_____

XOXO

Do you like to receive letters? Why? _____

_____

_____

Why do we often begin letters with "Dear"? _____

_____

_____

Explain the expression "happy as a clam." _____

_____

_____

_____

Why does XOXO mean kisses and hugs?

_____

_____

_____

_____

_____

_____

_____

Animal Talk

Describe how some animals communicate. _____

_____

_____

Describe three ways people can communicate without talking.

_____

_____

_____

If you could choose any animal to talk to, which animal would you choose and what questions would you ask?

_____

_____

_____

OINK   HELLO

Why don't animals speak our language?

_____

_____

_____

_____

_____

_____

_____

© McGraw-Hill Children's Publishing   IF5027 *Guided Writing*

Name_____

Get Moving

Why do you suppose our arms and legs often go to sleep while we are still awake?

_____

_____

How do you think people woke up before alarm clocks were invented?

_____

_____

Why do we often look in the mirror while brushing our teeth?

_____

_____

_____

YAWN

How long do you need to sleep to feel rested and ready for a new day? Why?

_____

_____

_____

_____

_____

_____

Keeping Cool

What might explain why penguins don't freeze in the cold?

_____

_____

Describe five things people do to keep warm. _____

_____

_____

Why do some people like to be warm and others cool? _____

_____

_____

_____

What is the best way to keep cool on a warm day?

_____

_____

_____

_____

_____

_____

_____